HAL•LEONARD

GUITAR
PLAY·ALONG®

VOL. 168

TAYLOR SWIFT

Photo courtesy of Big Machine Label Group

ISBN 978-1-4803-2161-8

HAL•LEONARD®
CORPORATION

7777 W. BLUEMOUND RD. P.O. BOX 13819 MILWAUKEE, WI 53213

Visit Hal Leonard Online at
www.halleonard.com

Guitar Notation Legend

THE MUSICAL STAFF shows pitches and rhythms and is divided by bar lines into measures. Pitches are named after the first seven letters of the alphabet.

TABLATURE graphically represents the guitar fingerboard. Each horizontal line represents a string, and each number represents a fret.

4th string, 2nd fret   1st & 2nd strings open, played together   open D chord

HALF-STEP BEND: Strike the note and bend up 1/2 step.

WHOLE-STEP BEND: Strike the note and bend up one step.

GRACE NOTE BEND: Strike the note and immediately bend up as indicated.

SLIGHT (MICROTONE) BEND: Strike the note and bend up 1/4 step.

BEND AND RELEASE: Strike the note and bend up as indicated, then release back to the original note. Only the first note is struck.

PRE-BEND: Bend the note as indicated, then strike it.

VIBRATO: The string is vibrated by rapidly bending and releasing the note with the fretting hand.

PALM MUTING: The note is partially muted by the pick hand lightly touching the string(s) just before the bridge.

HAMMER-ON: Strike the first (lower) note with one finger, then sound the higher note (on the same string) with another finger by fretting it without picking.

PULL-OFF: Place both fingers on the notes to be sounded. Strike the first note and without picking, pull the finger off to sound the second (lower) note.

LEGATO SLIDE: Strike the first note and then slide the same fret-hand finger up or down to the second note. The second note is not struck.

SHIFT SLIDE: Same as legato slide, except the second note is struck.

TRILL: Very rapidly alternate between the notes indicated by continuously hammering on and pulling off.

TAPPING: Hammer ("tap") the fret indicated with the pick-hand index or middle finger and pull off to the note fretted by the fret hand.

NATURAL HARMONIC: Strike the note while the fret-hand lightly touches the string directly over the fret indicated.

PINCH HARMONIC: The note is fretted normally and a harmonic is produced by adding the edge of the thumb or the tip of the index finger of the pick hand to the normal pick attack.

TREMOLO PICKING: The note is picked as rapidly and continuously as possible.

VIBRATO BAR DIVE AND RETURN: The pitch of the note or chord is dropped a specified number of steps (in rhythm), then returned to the original pitch.

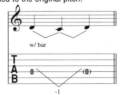

VIBRATO BAR SCOOP: Depress the bar just before striking the note, then quickly release the bar.

VIBRATO BAR DIP: Strike the note and then immediately drop a specified number of steps, then release back to the original pitch.

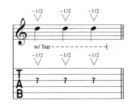

Additional Musical Definitions

(accent)   • Accentuate note (play it louder).

(staccato)   • Play the note short.

D.S. al Coda   • Go back to the sign (𝄋), then play until the measure marked "*To Coda*," then skip to the section labelled "**Coda**."

D.C. al Fine   • Go back to the beginning of the song and play until the measure marked "*Fine*" (end).

Fill   • Label used to identify a brief melodic figure which is to be inserted into the arrangement.

N.C.   • Harmony is implied.

• Repeat measures between signs.

• When a repeated section has different endings, play the first ending only the first time and the second ending only the second time.

CONTENTS

Back to December

Words and Music by Taylor Swift

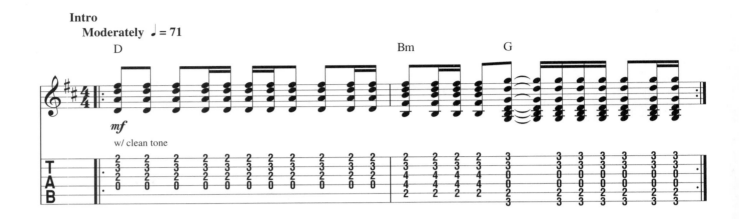

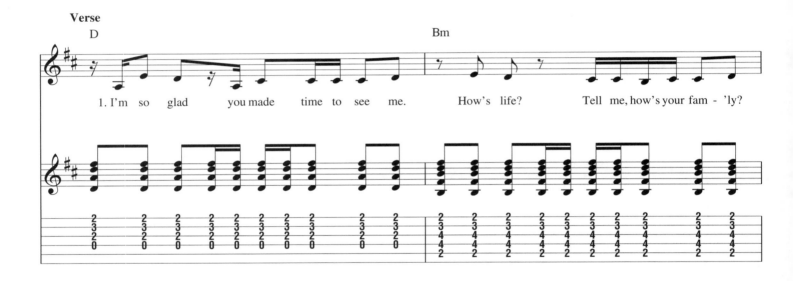

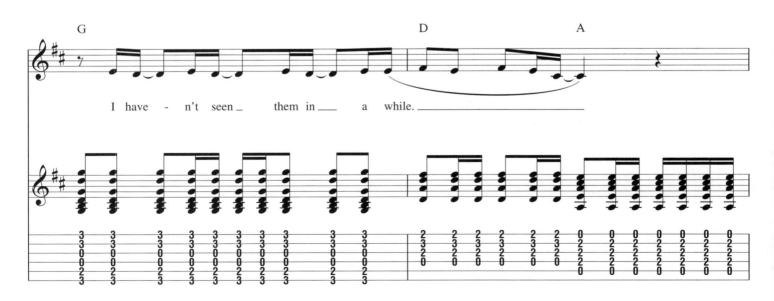

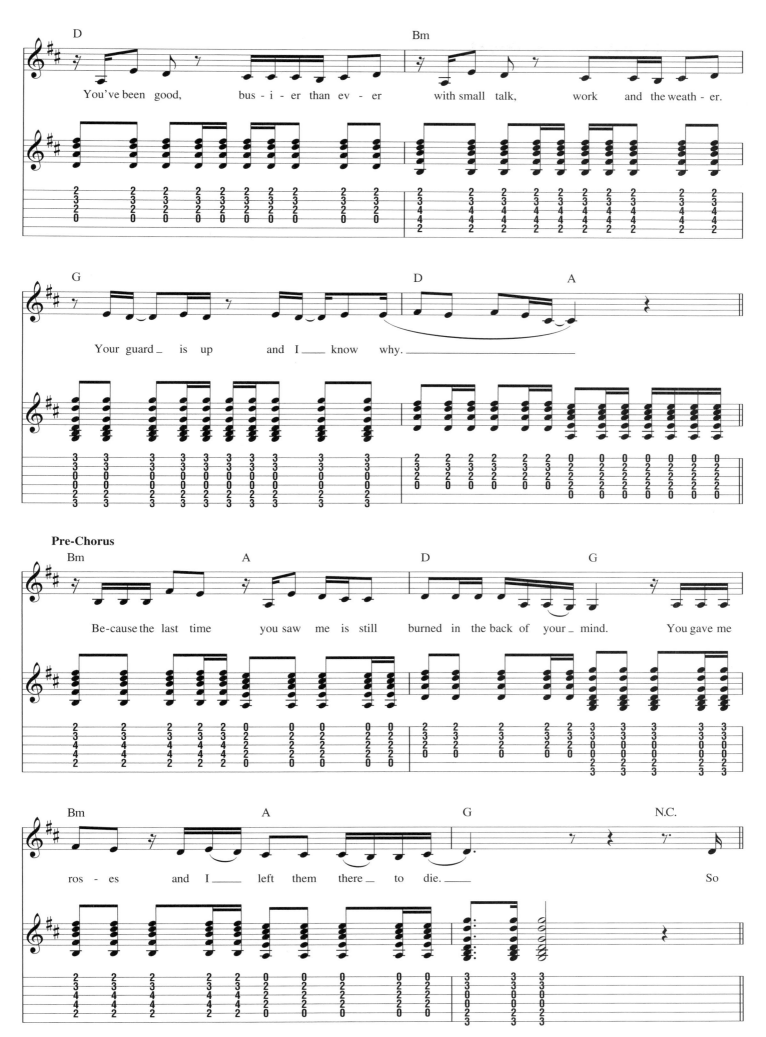

think a-bout sum-mer, all the beau-ti-ful times _ I watched you laugh-in' from the pas-sen-ger side and

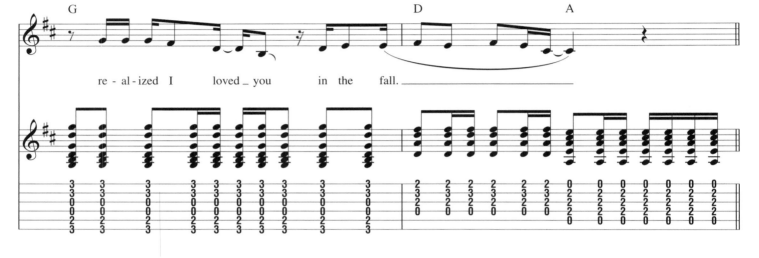

re-al-ized I loved _ you in the fall. _

Pre-Chorus

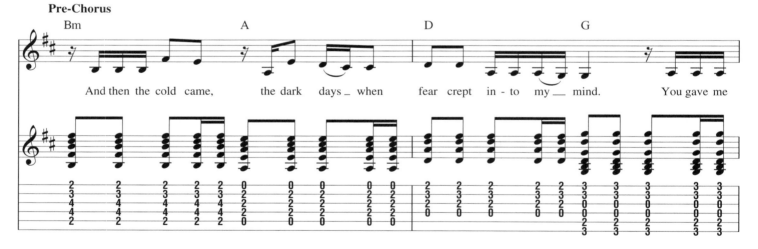

And then the cold came, the dark days _ when fear crept in-to my _ mind. You gave me

D.S. al Coda

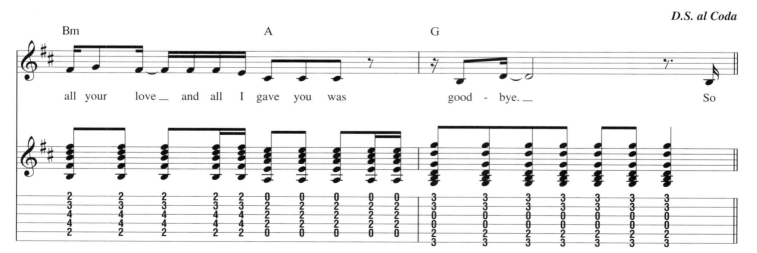

all your love _ and all I gave you was good-bye. _ So

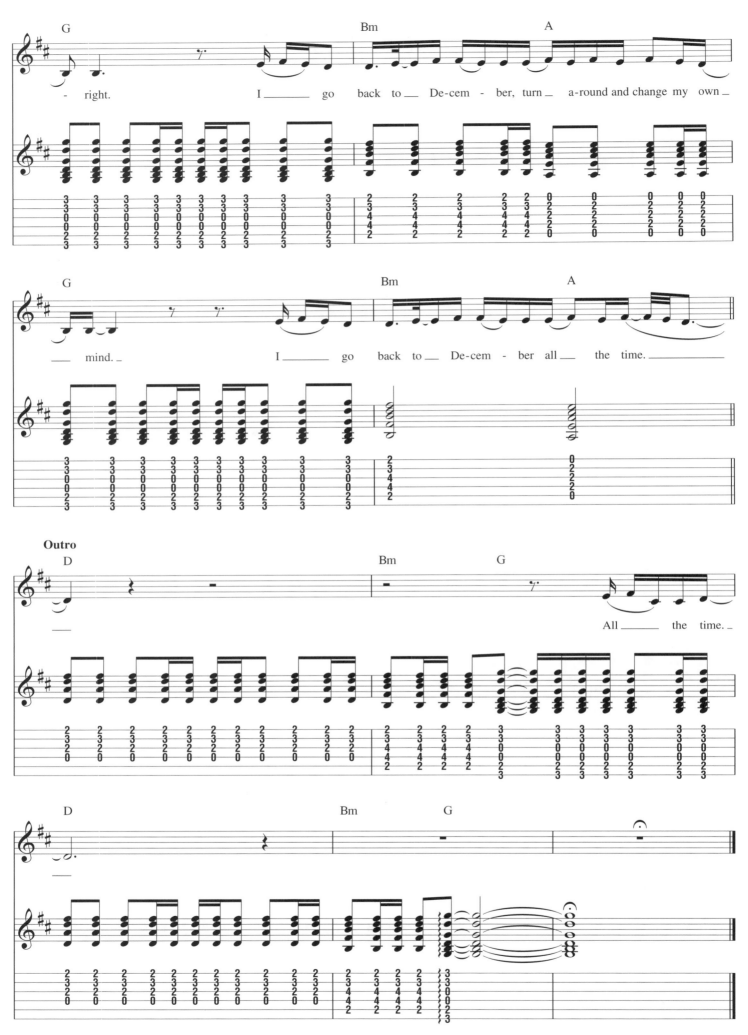

Picture to Burn

Words and Music by Taylor Swift and Liz Rose

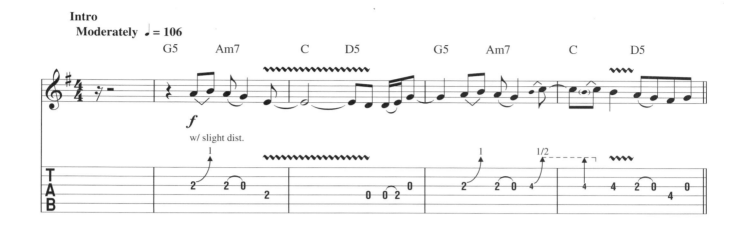

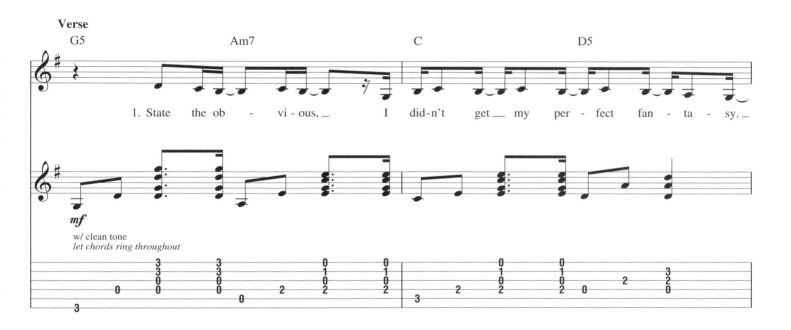

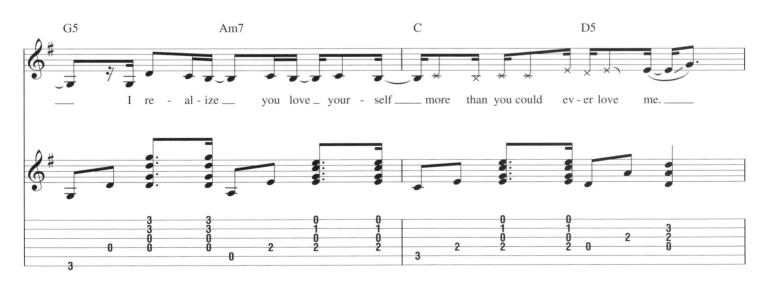

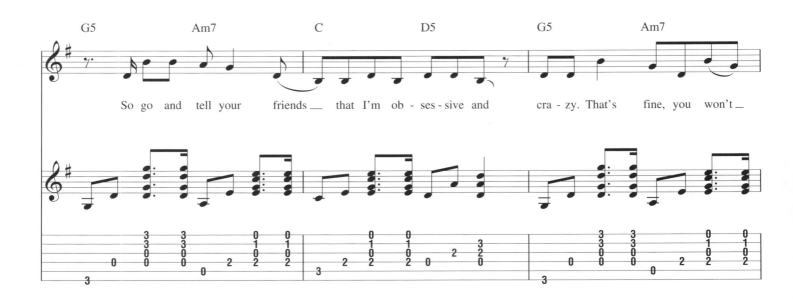

So go and tell your friends ___ that I'm ob - ses - sive and cra - zy. That's fine, you won't ___

mind if I say. ___ And by the way, ___ I hate ___ that

%̄ Chorus

stu - pid old pick - up truck you nev - er let me drive. You're a red - neck heart - break who's

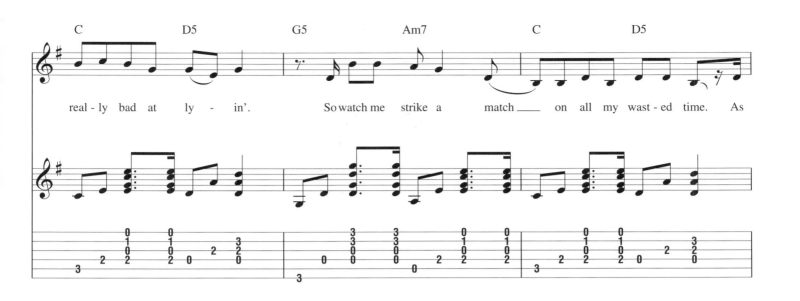

real - ly bad at ly - in'. So watch me strike a match ___ on all my wast - ed time. As

To Coda 1
To Coda 2

Interlude

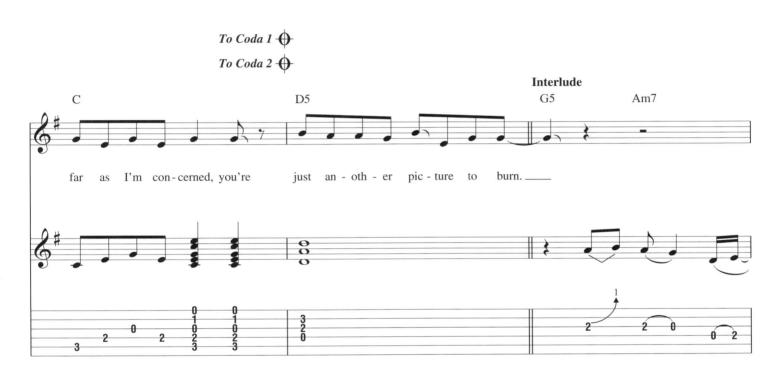

far as I'm con - cerned, you're just an - oth - er pic - ture to burn. ___

Verse

2. There's no time ___ for tears, ___ I'm just sit - tin' here ___ plan - nin' my ___ re - venge. ___

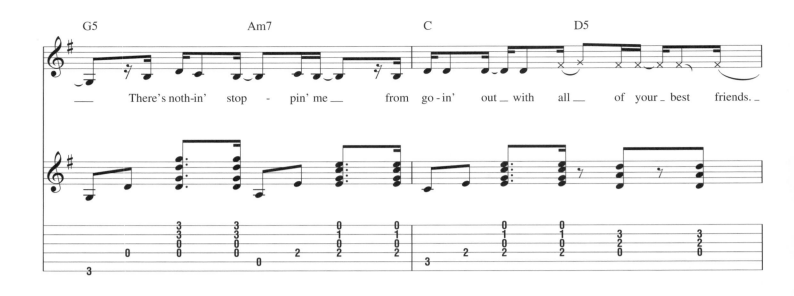

There's noth-in' stop - pin' me ___ from go-in' out ___ with all ___ of your ___ best friends. ___

And if you come a - round ___ say-in' sor-ry to me, my dad-dy's gon-na show you how

⊕ Coda 1

D.S. al Coda 1

sor - ry you'll be. 'Cause I hate that

just an - oth - er pic - ture to burn. ___

Guitar/Banjo Solo

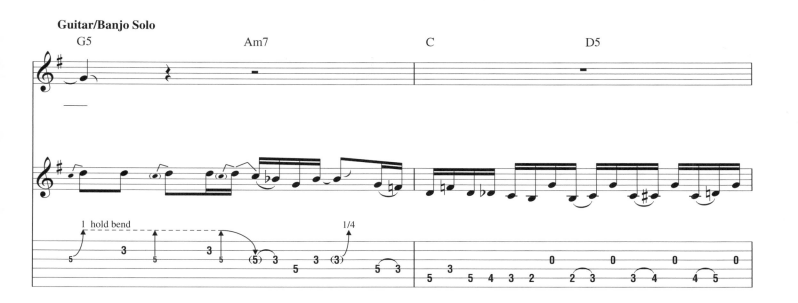

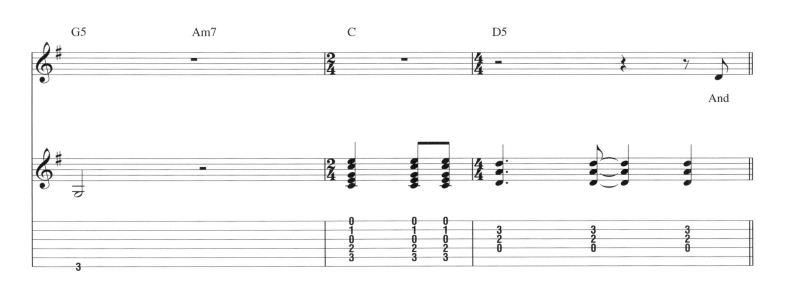

And

Bridge

if you're miss - in' me, you bet - ter keep it to your - self _____ 'cause

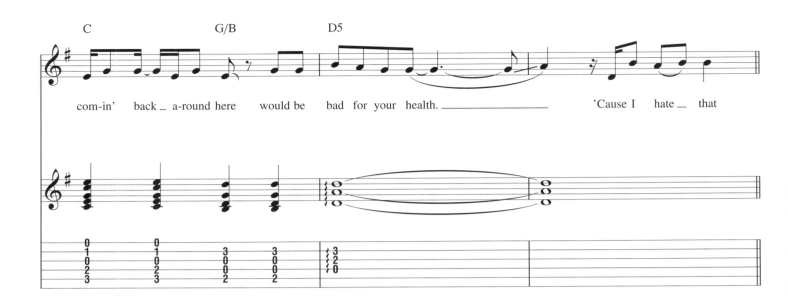

com-in' back __ a-round here would be bad for your health. _____ 'Cause I hate __ that

Chorus

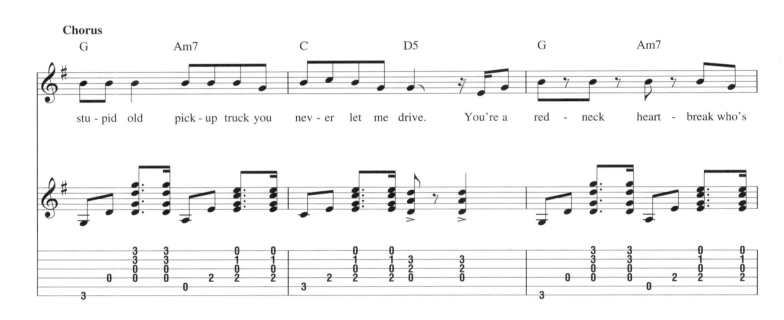

stu - pid old pick - up truck you nev - er let me drive. You're a red - neck heart - break who's

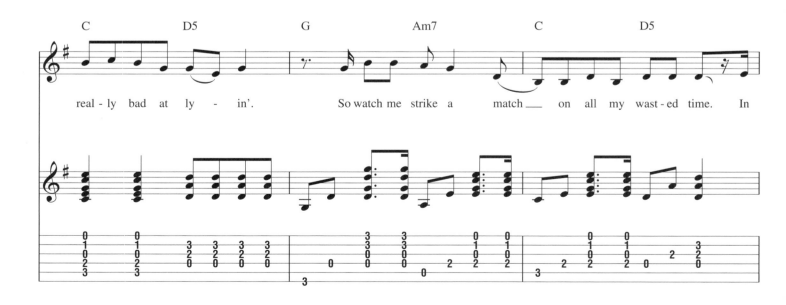

real - ly bad at ly - in'. So watch me strike a match __ on all my wast - ed time. In

Coda 2

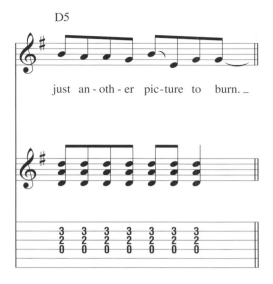

Outro

Eyes Open

from THE HUNGER GAMES
Words and Music by Taylor Swift

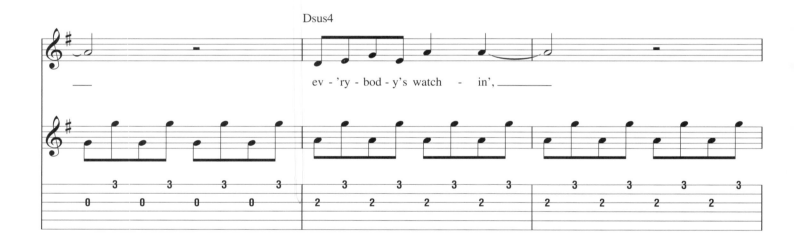

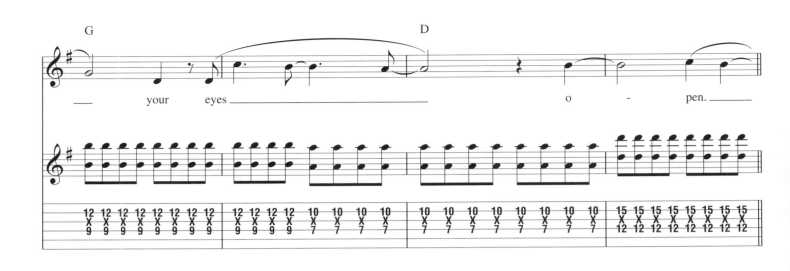

Chorus

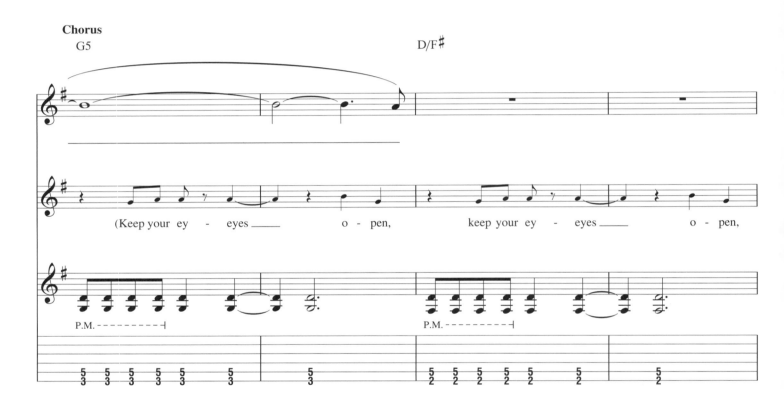

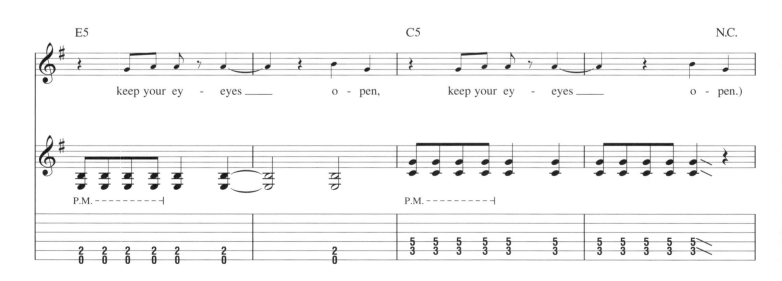

Mean

Words and Music by Taylor Swift

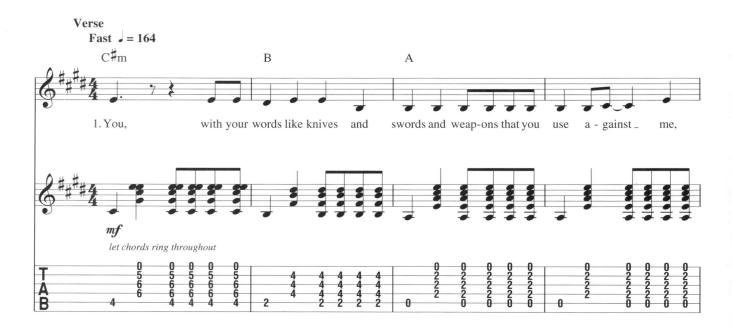

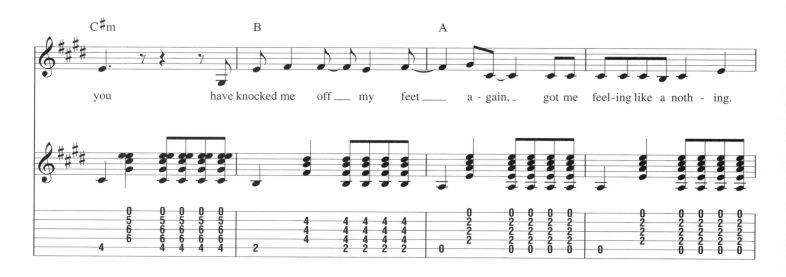

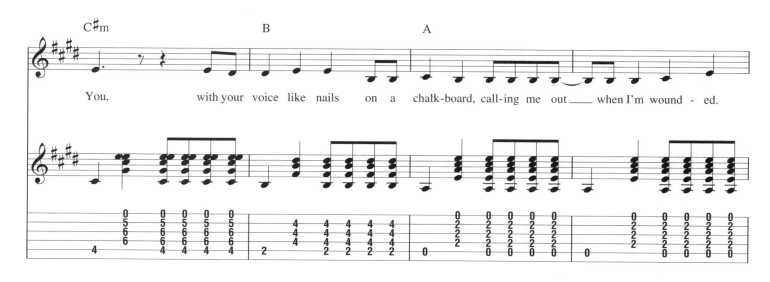

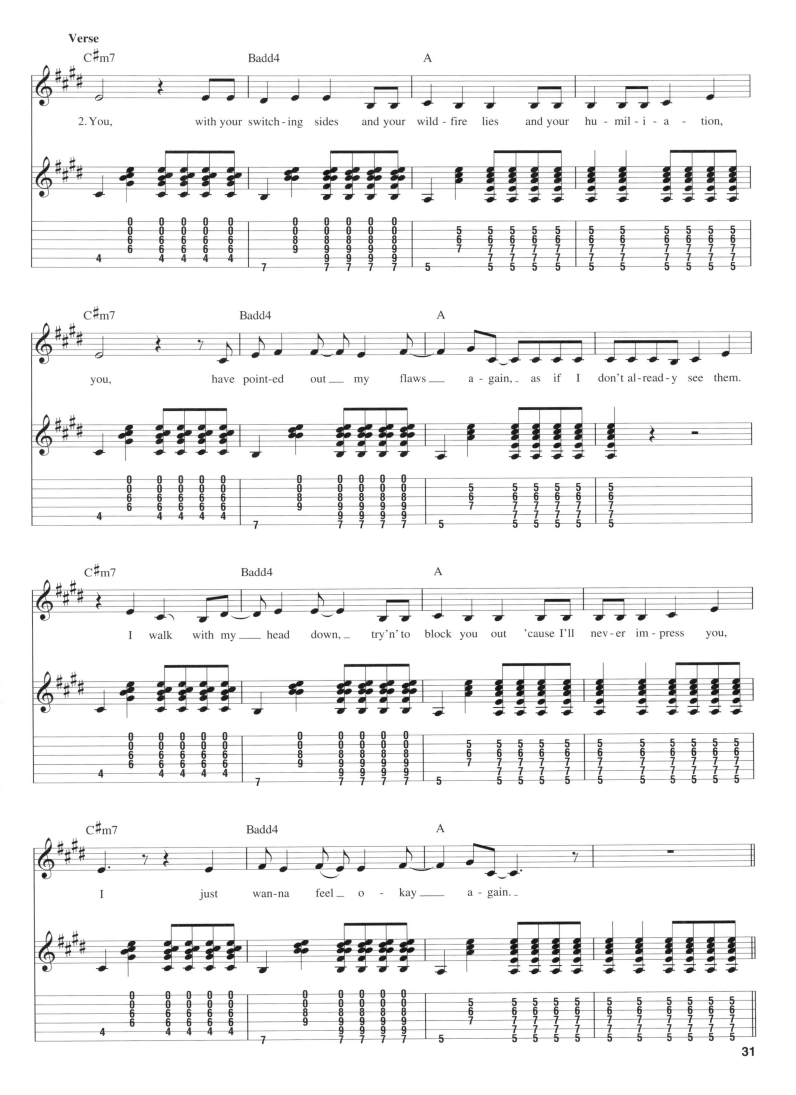

Ours

Words and Music by Taylor Swift

Capo V

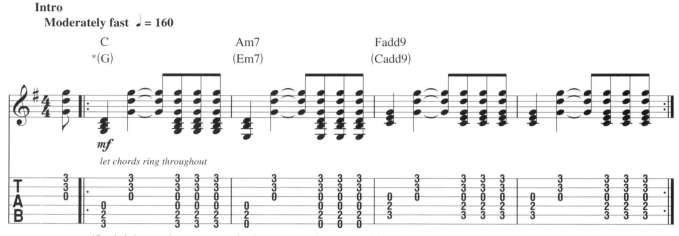

*Symbols in parentheses represent chord names respective to capoed guitar.
Symbols above reflect actual sounding chords. Capoed fret is "0" in tab.

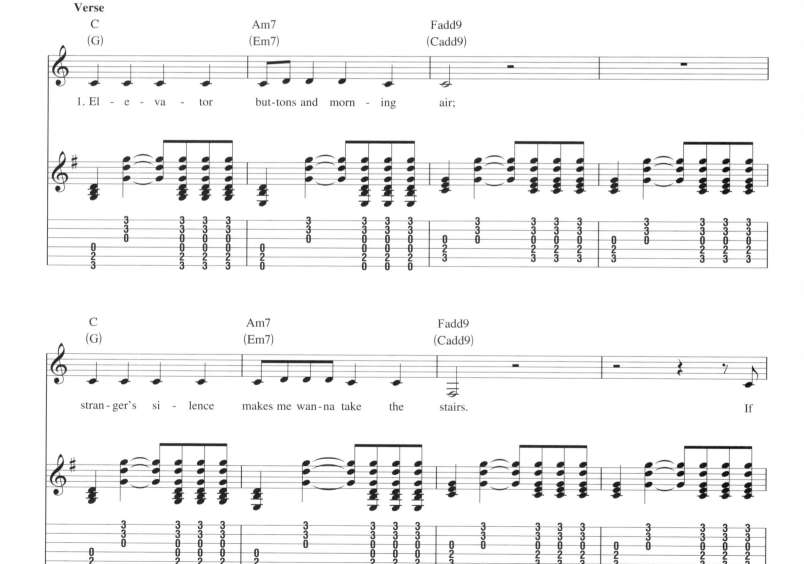

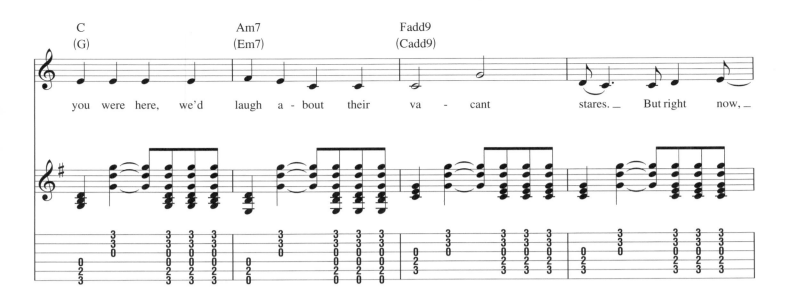

you were here, we'd laugh a - bout their va - cant stares. __ But right now, __

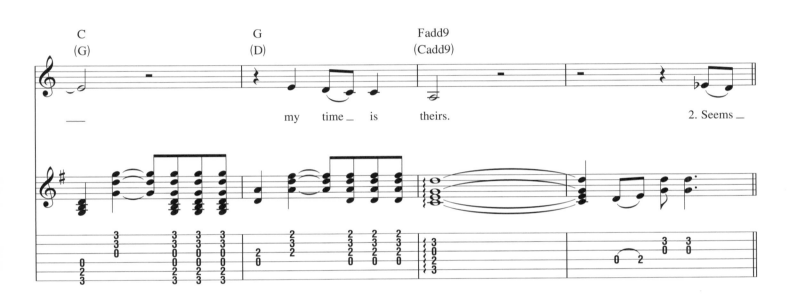

__ my time __ is theirs. 2. Seems __

𝄋 Verse

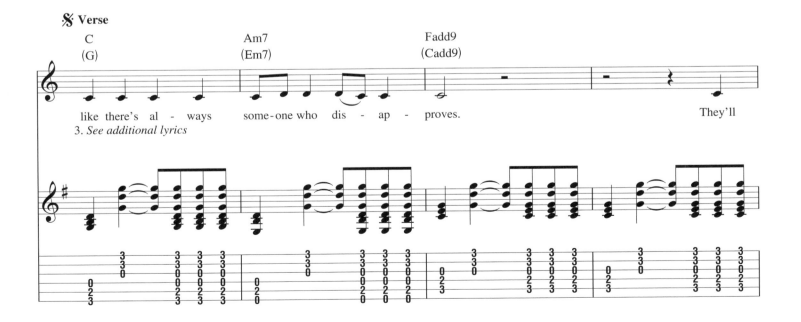

like there's al - ways some-one who dis - ap - proves. They'll
3. *See additional lyrics*

judge it like they know a-bout me ___ and you. And the

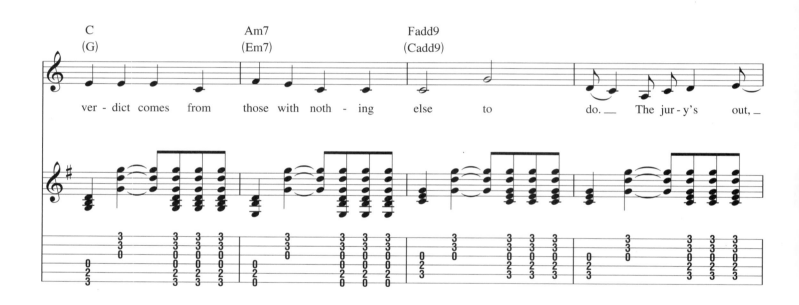

ver - dict comes from those with noth - ing else to do. ___ The jur - y's out, ___

To Coda ⊕

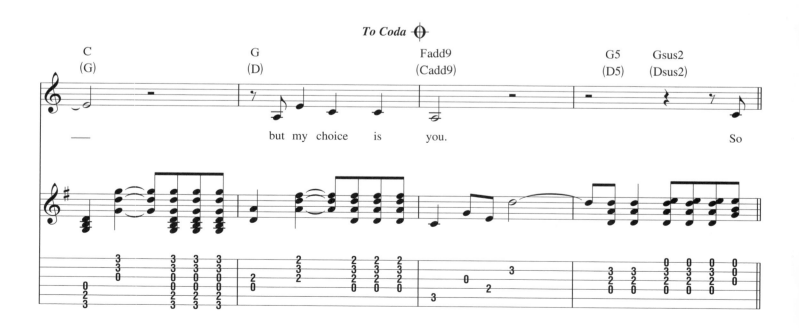

___ but my choice is you. So

Chorus

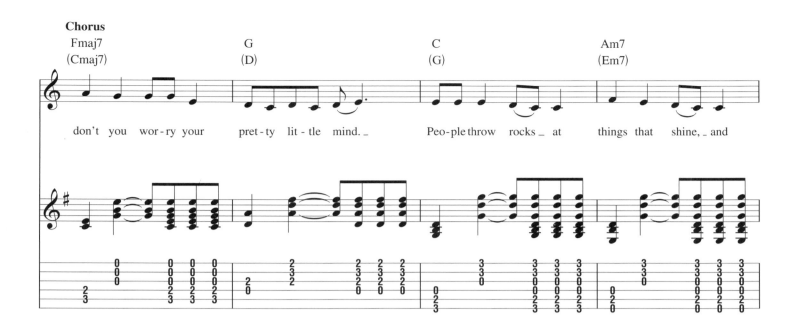

don't you wor-ry your pret-ty lit-tle mind. _ Peo-ple throw rocks _ at things that shine, _ and

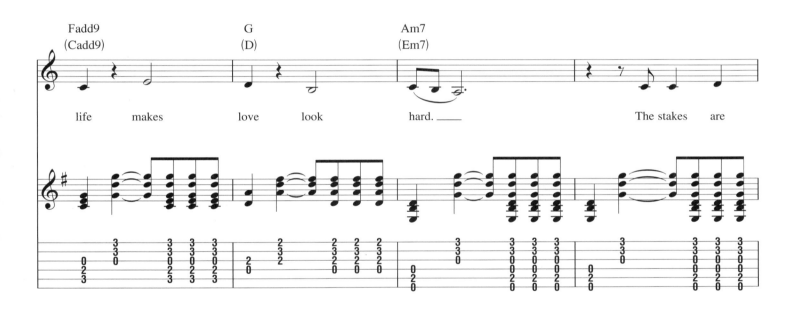

life makes love look hard. _____ The stakes are

high, the wa-ter's rough, but this love is

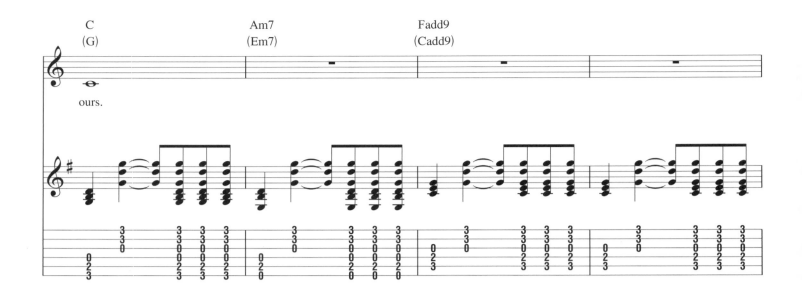

D.S. al Coda

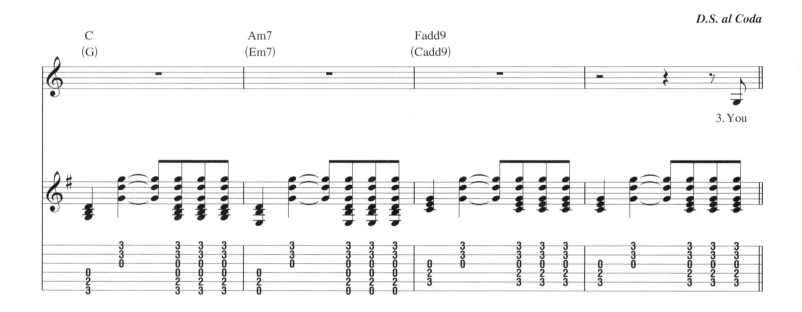

3. You

Coda

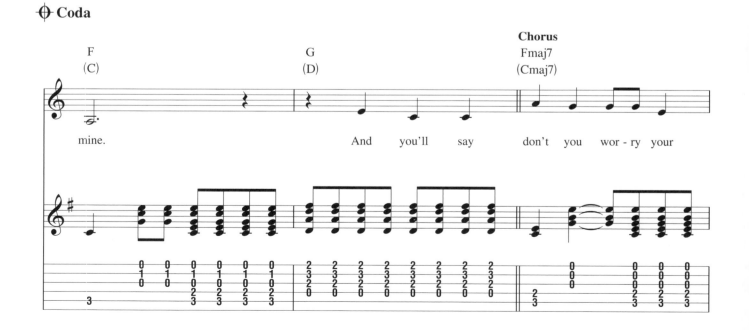

mine.   And   you'll   say   don't you wor-ry your

pret - ty lit - tle mind. _ Peo - ple throw rocks _ at things that shine, _ and

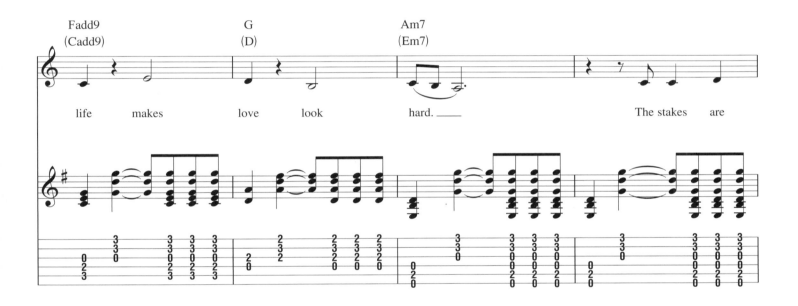

life makes love look hard. _____ The stakes are

high, the wa - ter's rough, but this love is

Interlude

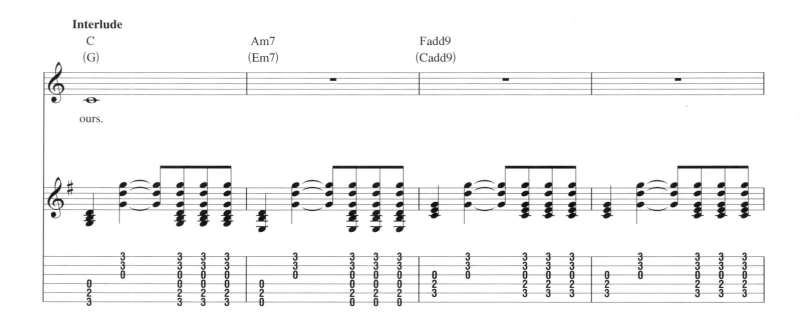

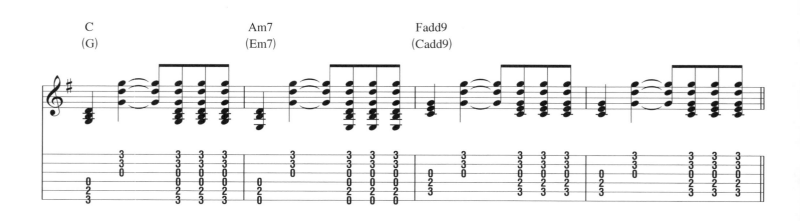

Bridge

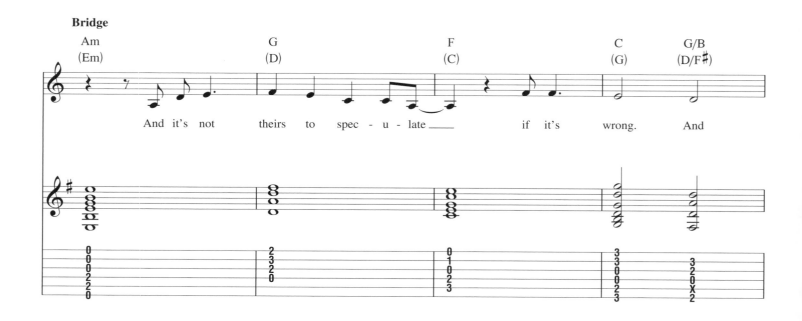

your hands are tough, but they _ are _ where _ mine be - long in.

I'll fight their doubt and give _ you _ faith _ with this song for

you.

Verse

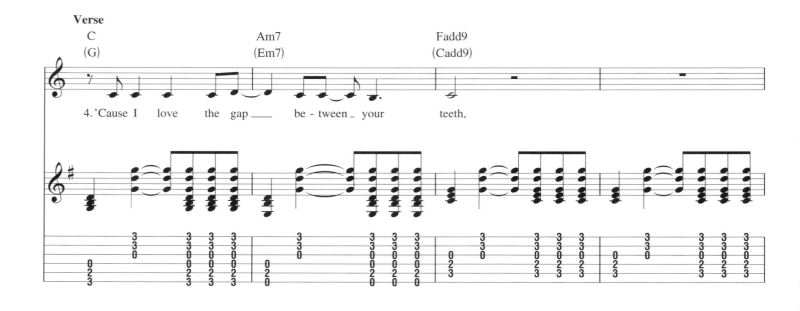

4.'Cause I love the gap ___ be - tween ___ your teeth,

and I love the rid-dles that ___ you speak. And an - y

snide re - marks ___ from my fa - ther a - bout your tat - toos ___ will be ig - nored ___

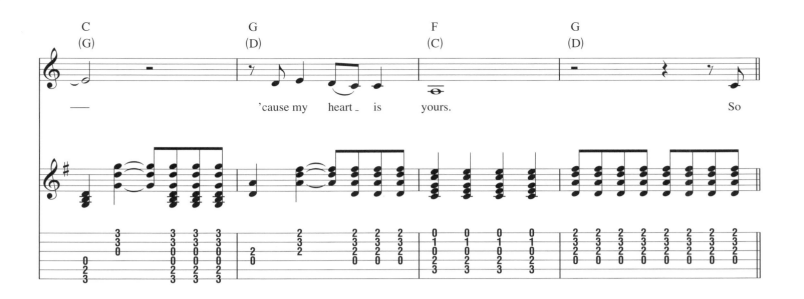

'cause my heart is yours. So

Chorus

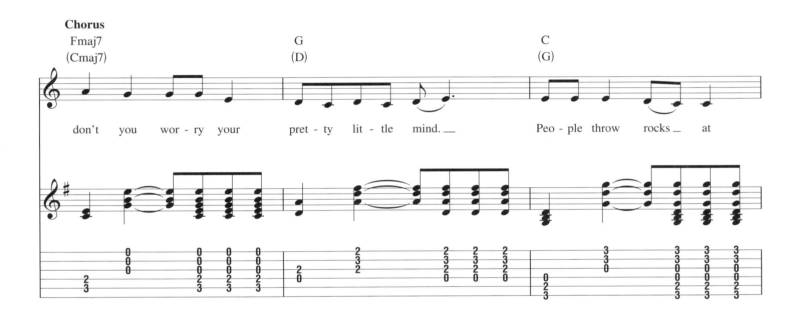

don't you wor-ry your pret-ty lit-tle mind. Peo-ple throw rocks at

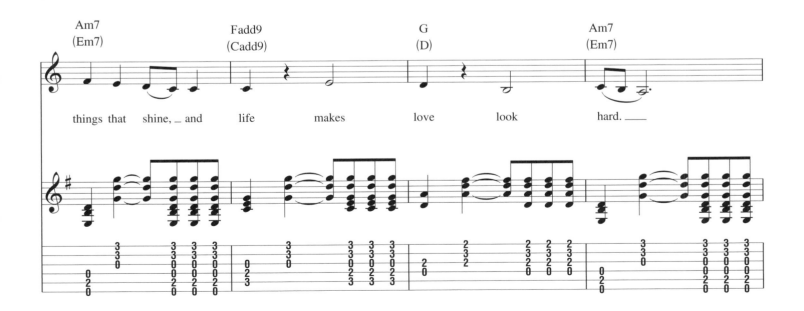

things that shine, and life makes love look hard.

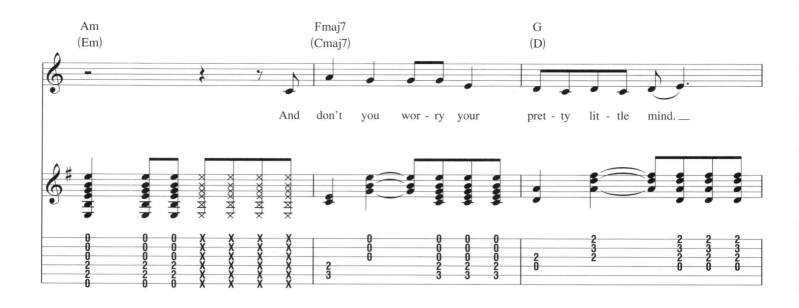

And don't you wor-ry your pret-ty lit-tle mind. __

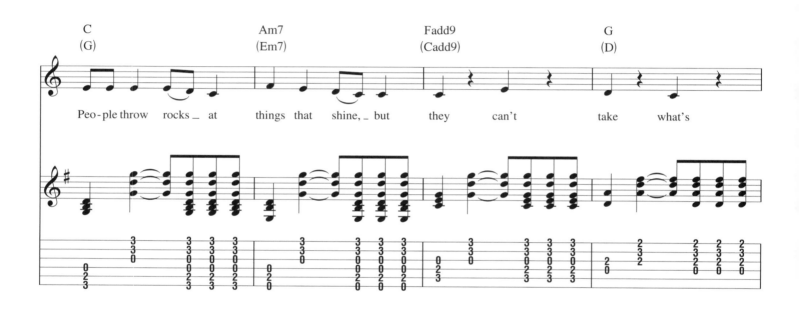

Peo-ple throw rocks __ at things that shine, __ but they can't take what's

ours. _____ They can't take what's

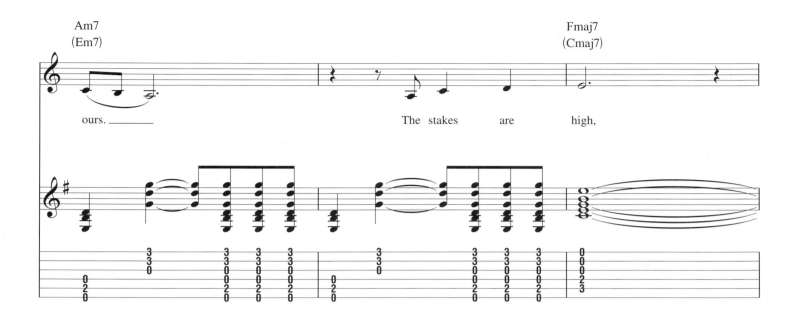

ours. _____ The stakes are high,

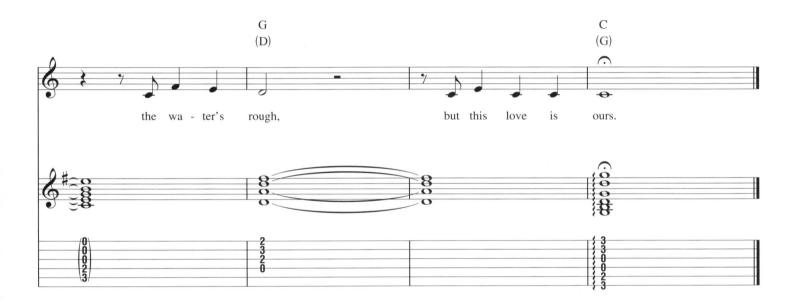

the wa-ter's rough, but this love is ours.

Additional Lyrics

3. You never know what people have up their sleeves.
   Ghosts from your past gonna jump out at me.
   Lurking in the shadows with their lip gloss smiles,
   But I don't care 'cause right now you're mine.
   And you'll say...

Sparks Fly

Words and Music by Taylor Swift

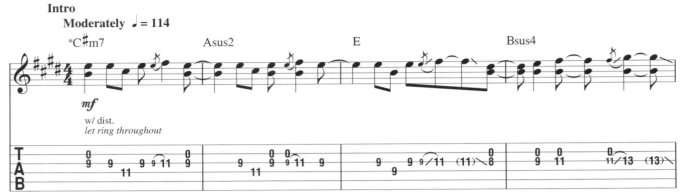

*To match original recording, tune up 1/2 step, or place capo at 1st fret.

1. The way you move is like a full-on rain-storm and I'm a house of cards. You're the

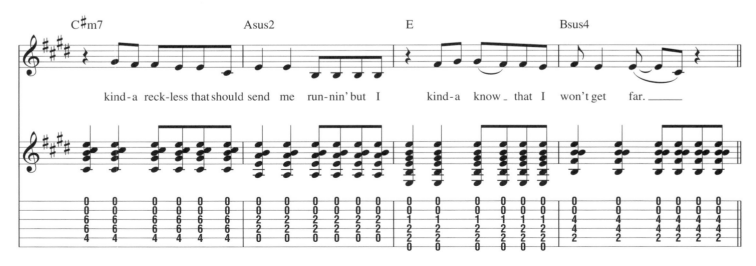

kind-a reck-less that should send me run-nin' but I kind-a know that I won't get far.

Pre-Chorus

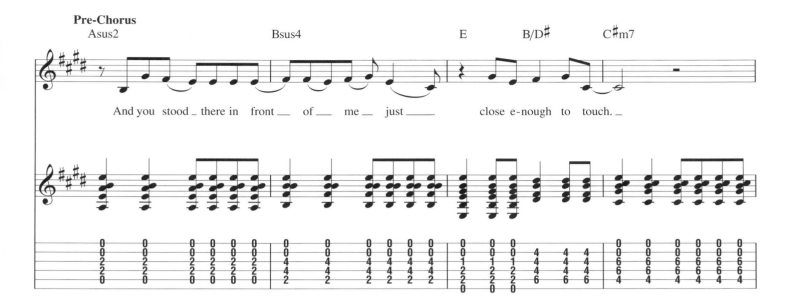

And you stood _ there in front _ of _ me _ just _____ close e-nough to touch. _

Close e-nough to hope ___ you could - n't _ see ___ what I was think-in' _ of. ___ Drop ev-'ry-thing

𝄋 Chorus

now. _ Meet _ me in the pour-ing rain. _ Kiss me on the side - walk, take a-way the pain. _ 'Cause

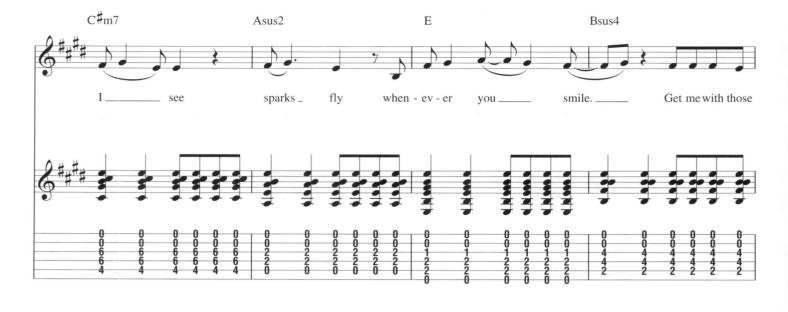

I _____ see sparks _ fly when-ev-er you _____ smile. _____ Get me with those

green _ eyes, ba-by, as the lights go down. Give me some-thin' that-'ll haunt me when _ you're not a-round. _ 'Cause

To Coda 1
To Coda 2

I _____ see sparks _ fly when-ev-er you _____ smile. _

Interlude

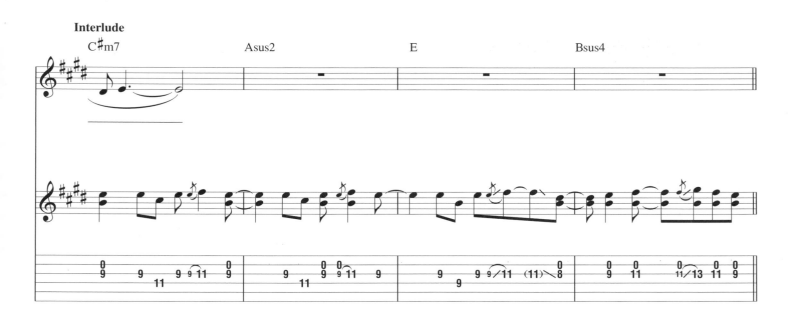

Verse

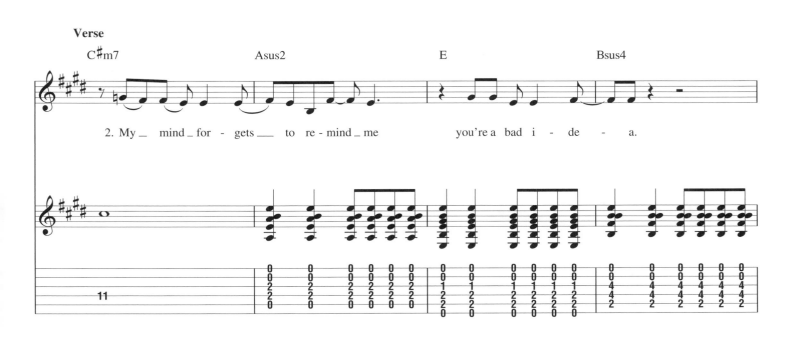

2. My _ mind _ for - gets _ to re - mind _ me   you're a bad i - de - a.

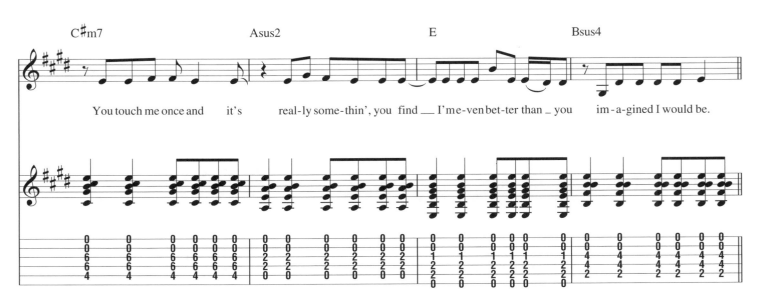

You touch me once and   it's   real-ly some-thin', you find _ I'm e-ven bet-ter than _ you   im - a - gined I would be.

I'm on my guard __ for the rest of the world __ but with you, __ I know it's no __ good.

D.S. al Coda 1

And I could __ wait pa - tient - ly __ but __ I real-ly wish you __ would __ drop ev-'ry-thing.

$\oplus$ **Coda 1**

Interlude

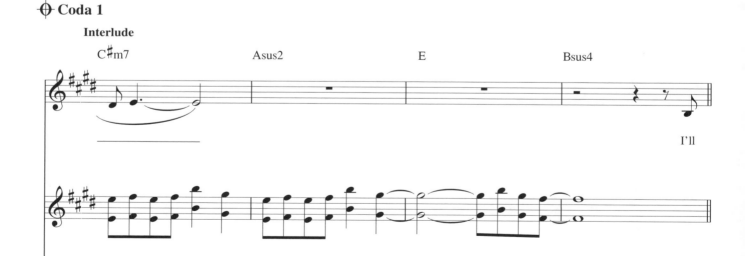

I'll

Bridge

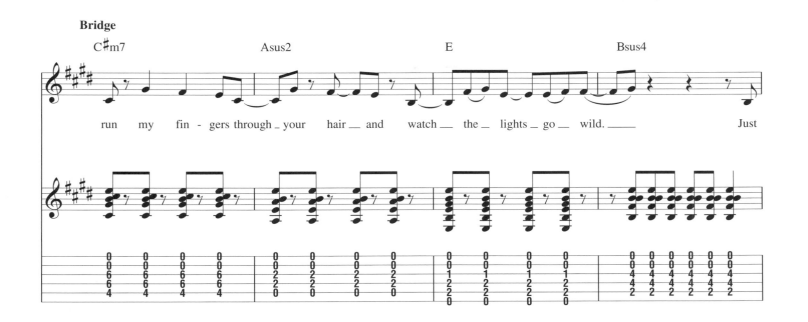

run my fin - gers through _ your hair _ and watch _ the _ lights _ go _ wild. _____ Just

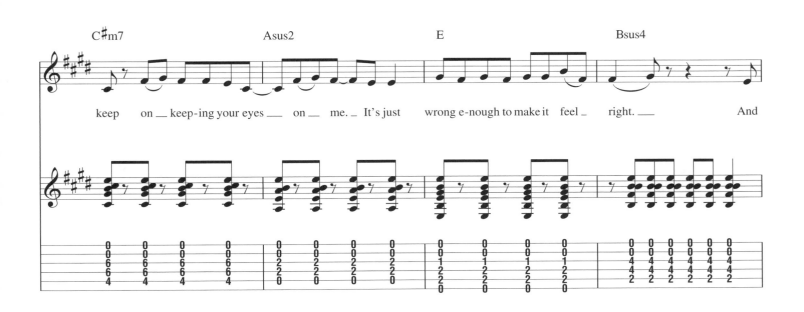

keep on _ keep-ing your eyes _____ on _ me. _ It's just wrong e-nough to make it feel _ right. _ And

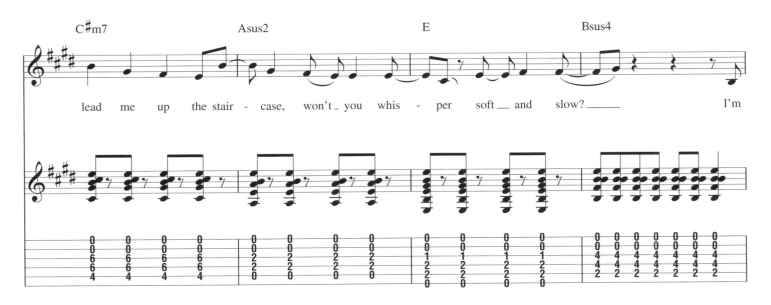

lead me up the stair - case, won't _ you whis - per soft _ and slow? _____ I'm

cap - tiv - at - ed by ____ you ba - by, like a fire - works ____ show. Drop ev - 'ry - thing

Chorus

now. Meet ____ me in the pour - ing rain. Kiss me on the side - walk, take a - way the pain. ____'Cause

D.S.S. al Coda 2

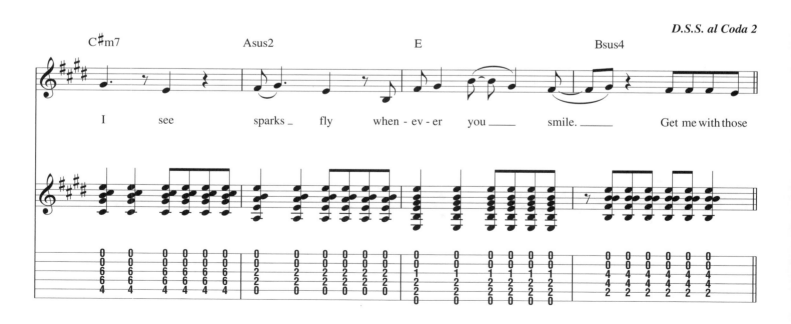

I see sparks ____ fly when - ev - er you ____ smile. ____ Get me with those

Coda 2

Outro

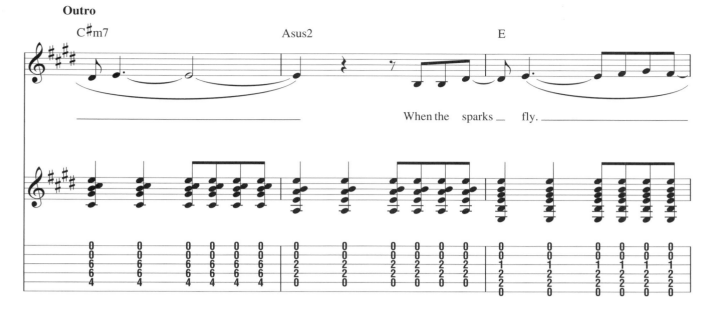

When the sparks __ fly. _____

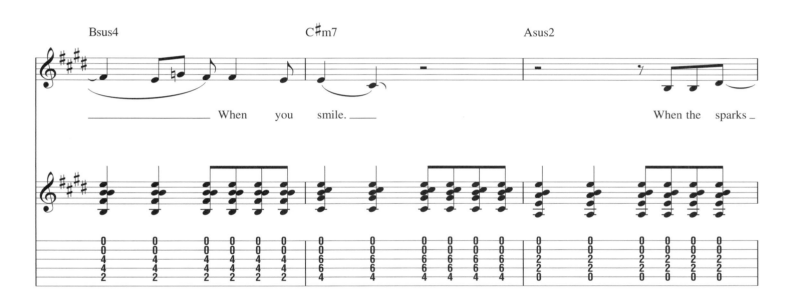

_____ When you smile. ____   When the sparks _

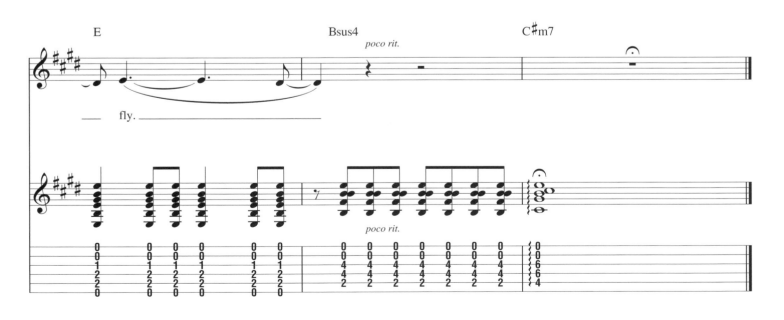

__ fly. _____

Red

Words and Music by Taylor Swift

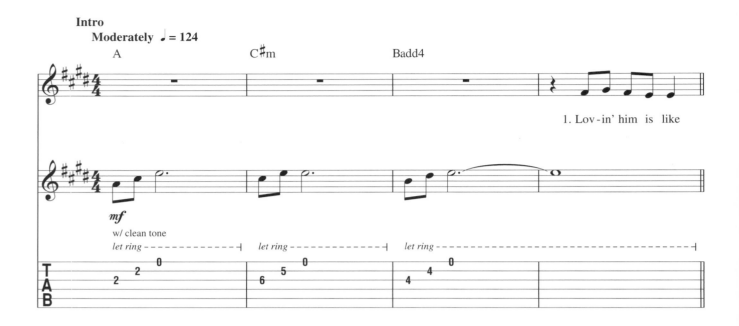

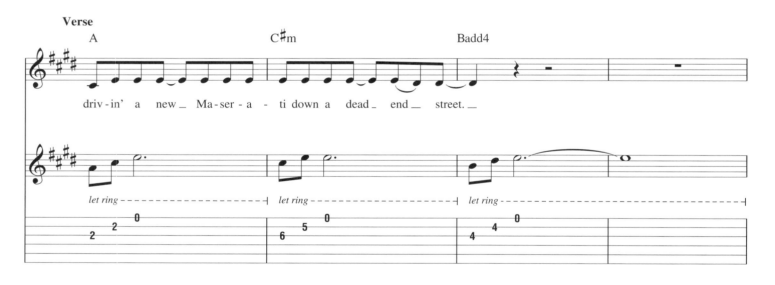

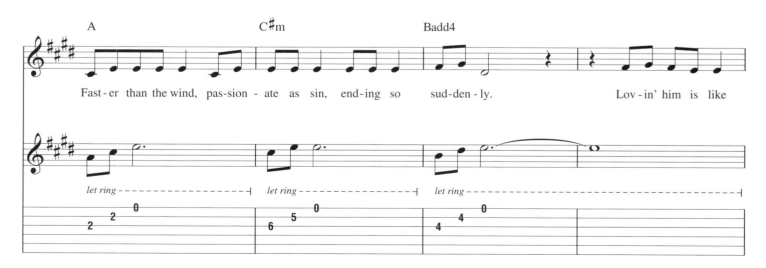

Chorus

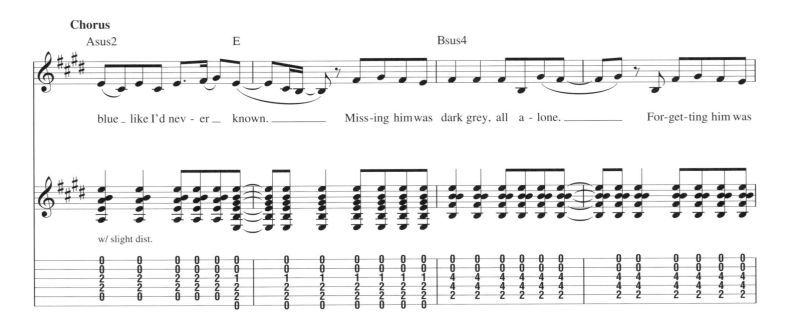

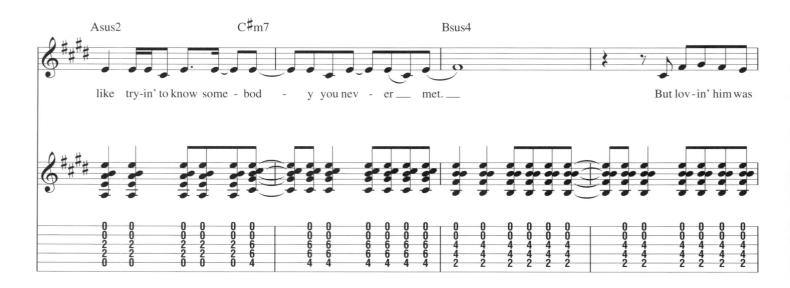

like try-in' to know some - bod — y you nev - er __ met. __

But lov-in' him was

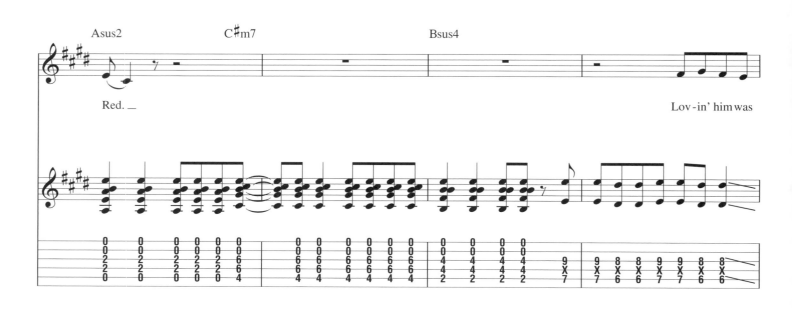

Red. __

Lov-in' him was

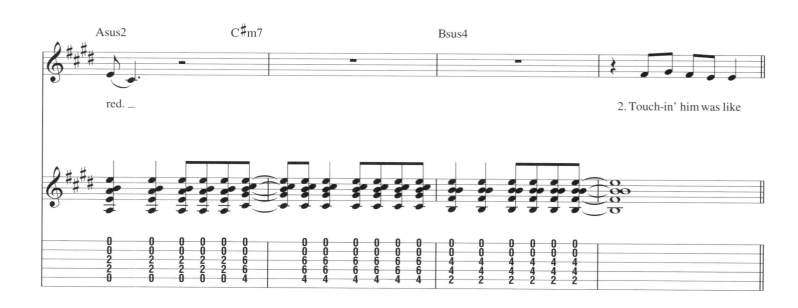

red. __

2. Touch-in' him was like

Verse

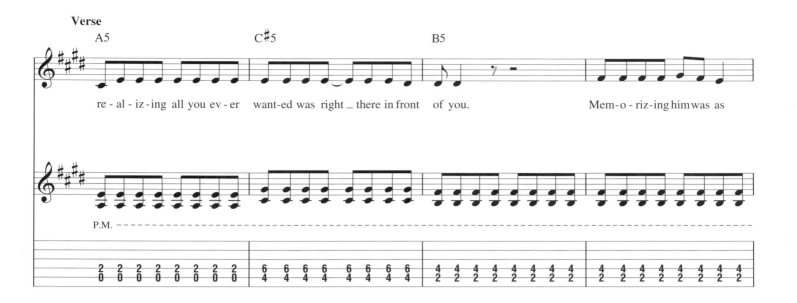

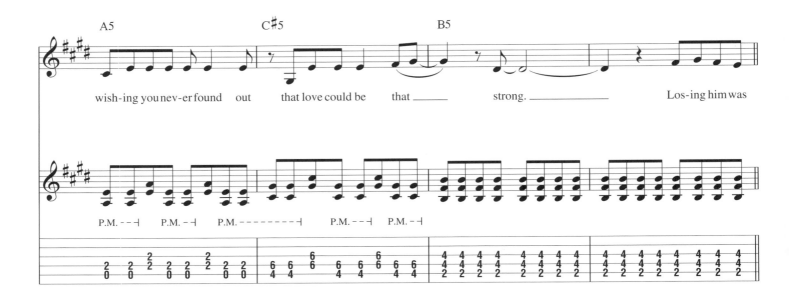

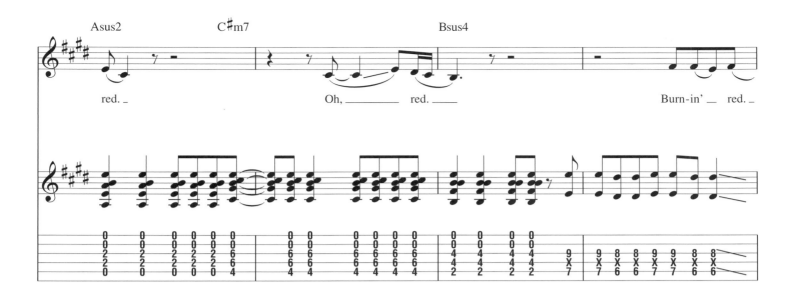

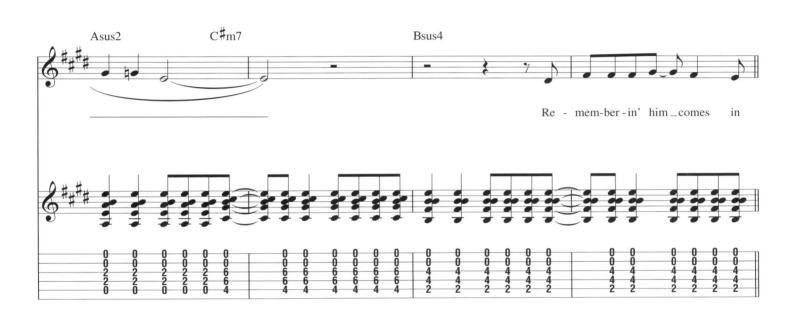

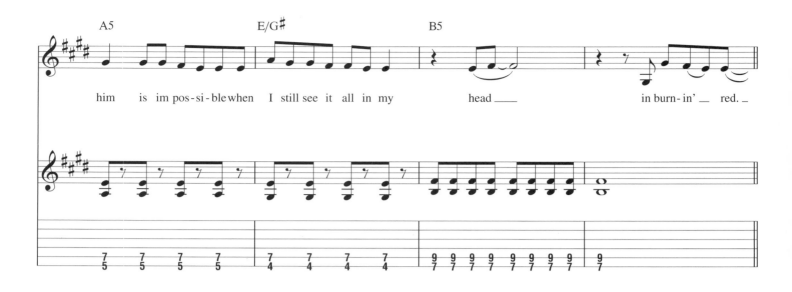

him is im-pos-si-ble when I still see it all in my head ___ in burn-in' ___ red. ___

Guitar Solo

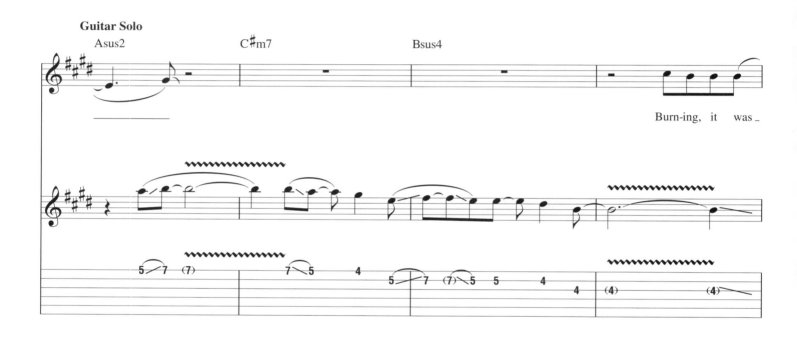

___ Burn-ing, it was ___

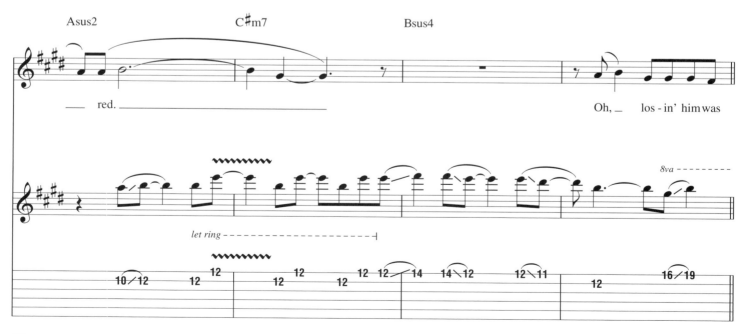

___ red. ___ Oh, ___ los-in' him was

Outro

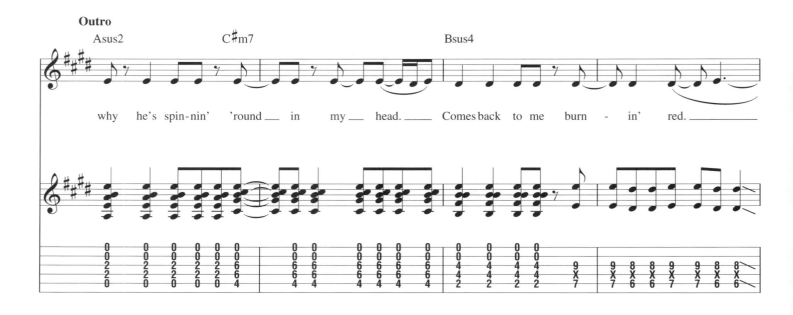

why he's spin-nin' 'round __ in my __ head. __ Comes back to me burn - in' red. _____

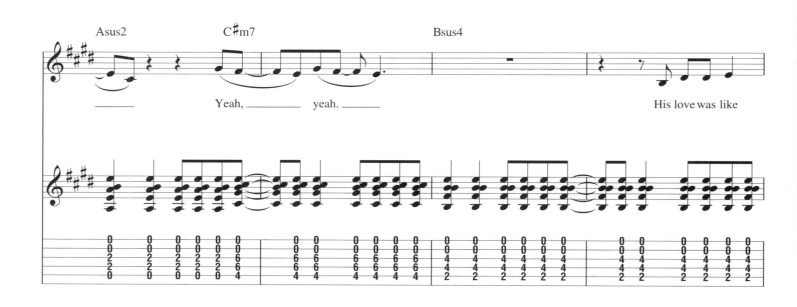

_____ Yeah, _____ yeah. _____ His love was like

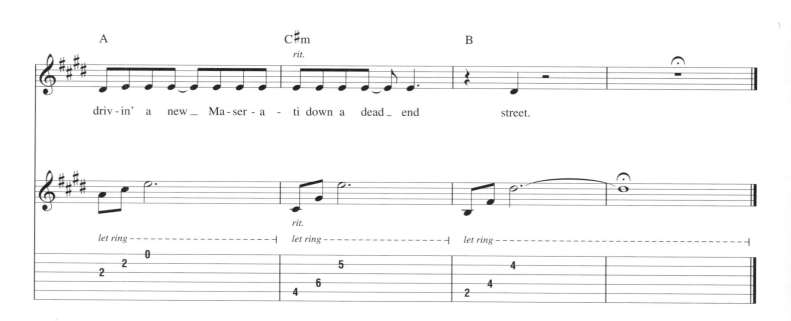

driv-in' a new __ Ma-ser-a - ti down a dead __ end street.

We Are Never Ever Getting Back Together

Words and Music by Taylor Swift, Shellback and Max Martin

Intro
Moderately ♩ = 86

*Knock on body of guitar.

Verse

1. I re-mem-ber when we broke _ up the first time. Say-ing, "This is it. I've had e-nough." 'Cause like, we

had-n't seen each oth-er in a month when you said you need-ed space. *Spoken:* What?

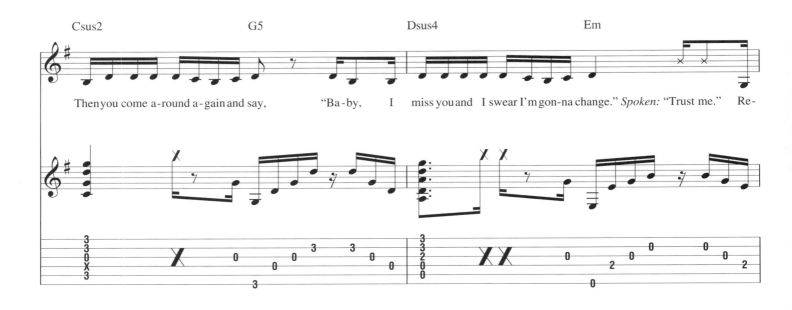

Then you come a-round a-gain and say, "Ba-by, I miss you and I swear I'm gon-na change." *Spoken:* "Trust me." Re-

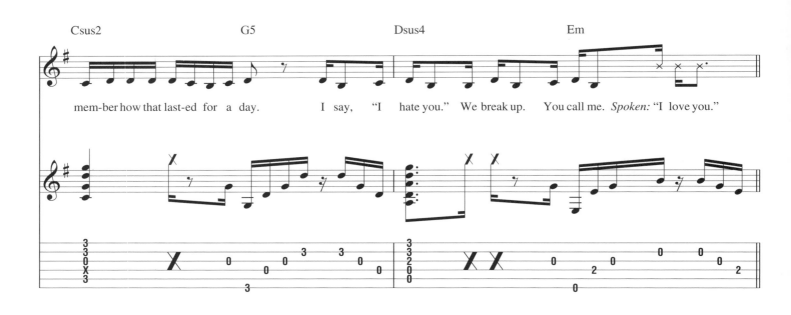

mem-ber how that last-ed for a day. I say, "I hate you." We break up. You call me. *Spoken:* "I love you."

Pre-Chorus

Oo, _____ oo, oo, ___ we called it off a-gain _ last night. ___ But

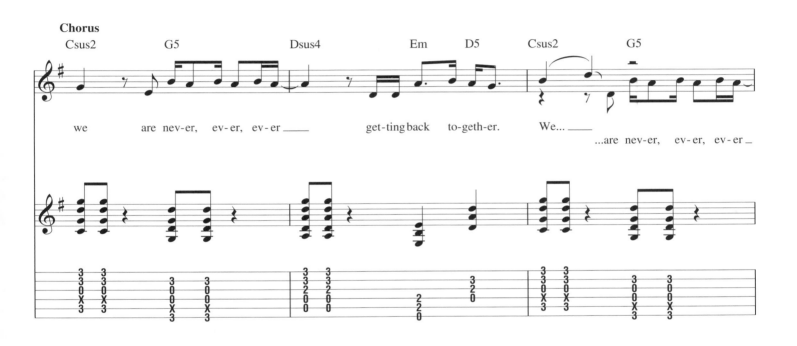

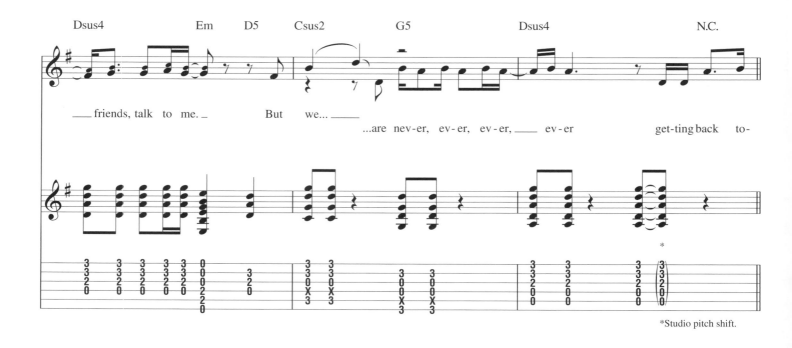

Dsus4   Em   D5   Csus2   G5   Dsus4   N.C.

___ friends, talk to me. _ But we... ___   ...are nev-er, ev-er, ev-er, ___ ev-er   get-ting back to-

*Studio pitch shift.

Interlude

Csus2   G5   Dsus4   Em

geth-er.   *Spoken:* Like, _   ev - er.   2. I'm

Verse

Csus2   G5   Dsus4   Em

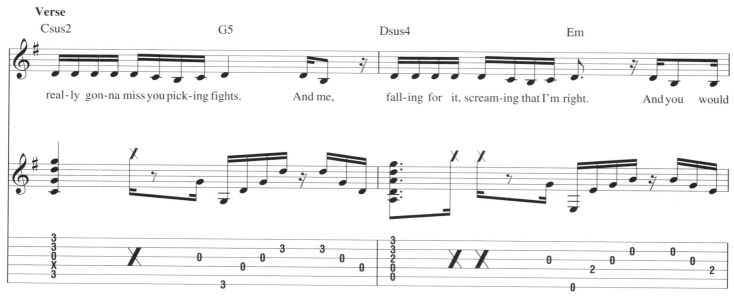

real-ly gon-na miss you pick-ing fights.   And me,   fall-ing for it, scream-ing that I'm right.   And you would

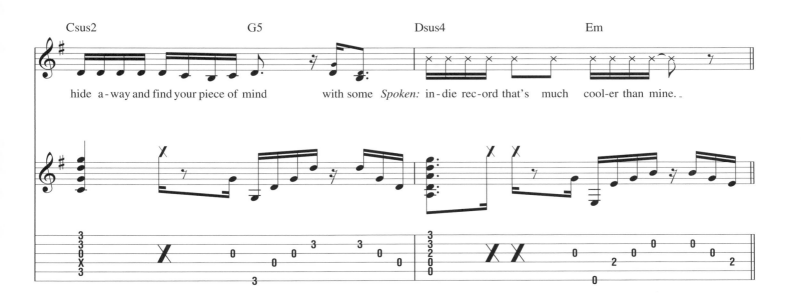

hide a-way and find your piece of mind with some *Spoken:* in-die rec-ord that's much cool-er than mine.

Pre-Chorus

Oo, _____ oo, oo, _____ you called me up a-gain to-night. ____ But

oo, _____ oo, oo, _____ this time I'm tell-ing you, I'm tell-ing you:

Chorus

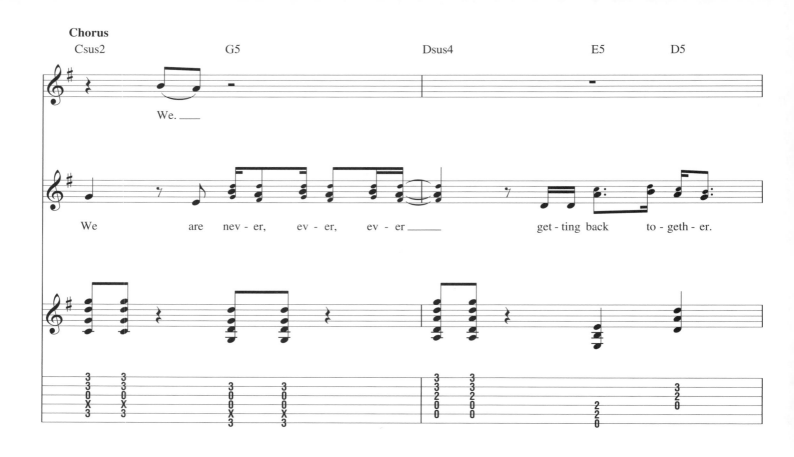

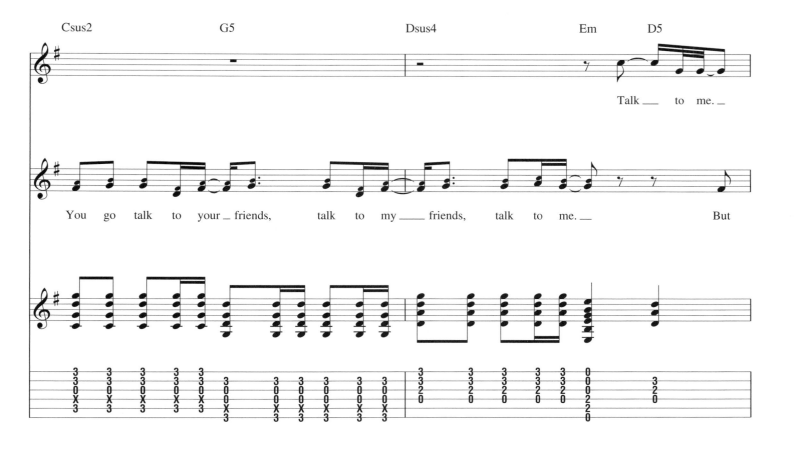

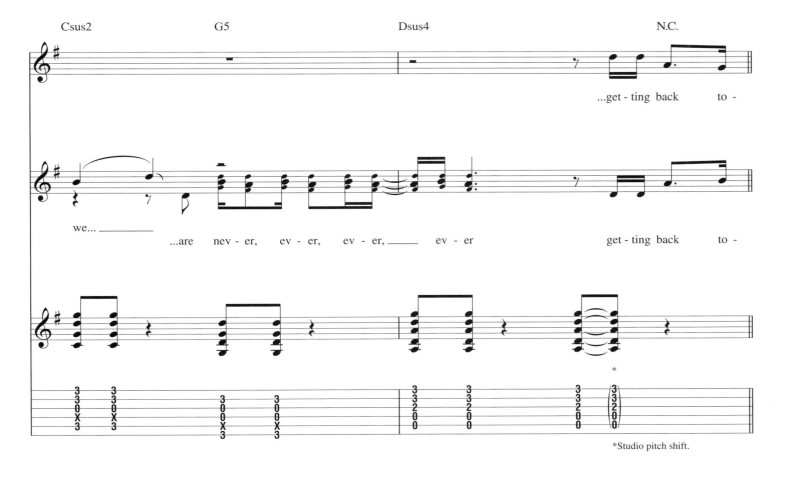

*Studio pitch shift.

Interlude

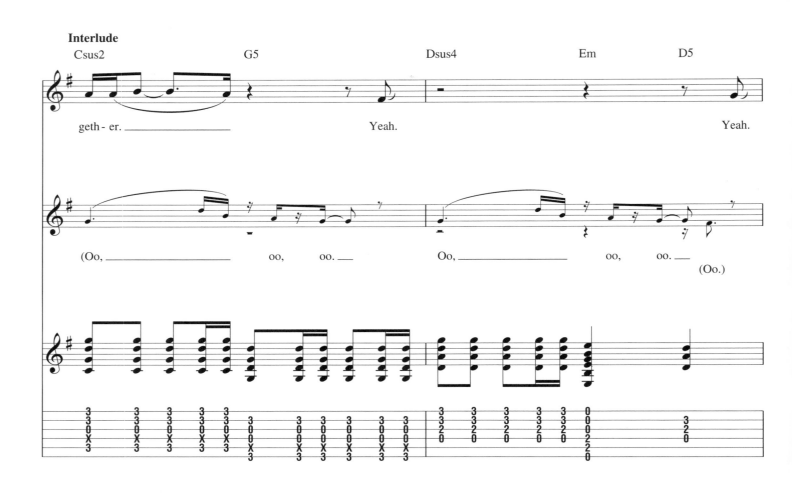

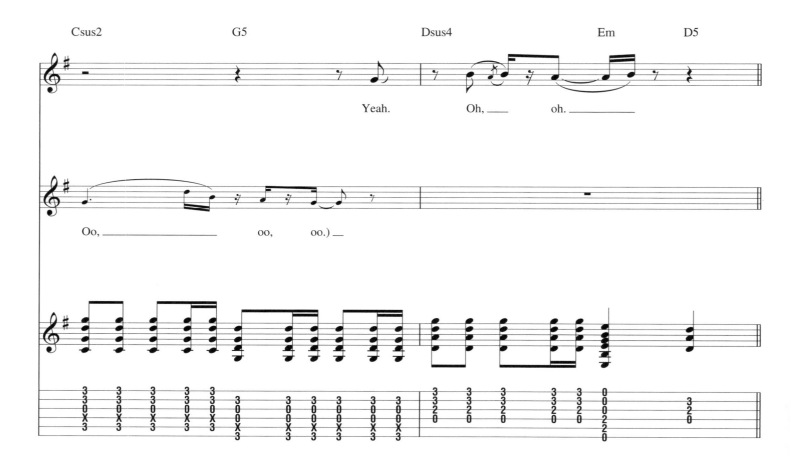

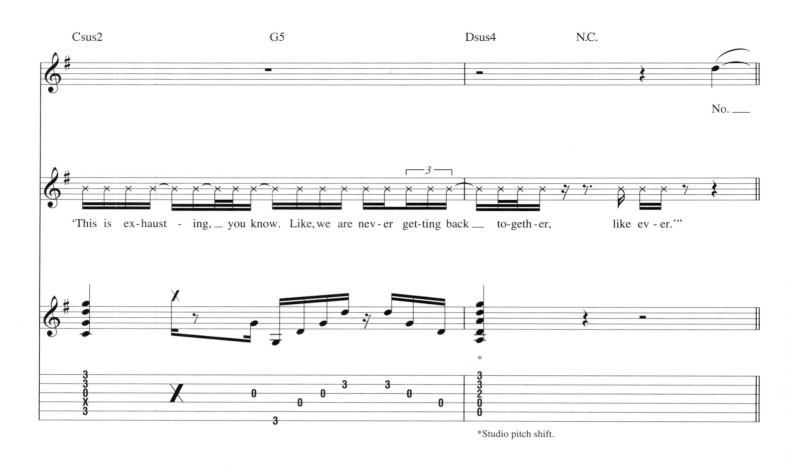

*Studio pitch shift.

Outro-Chorus

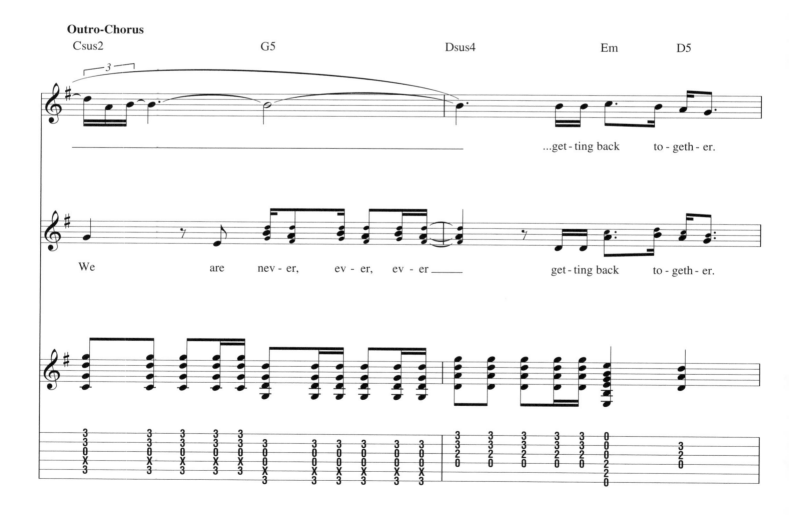

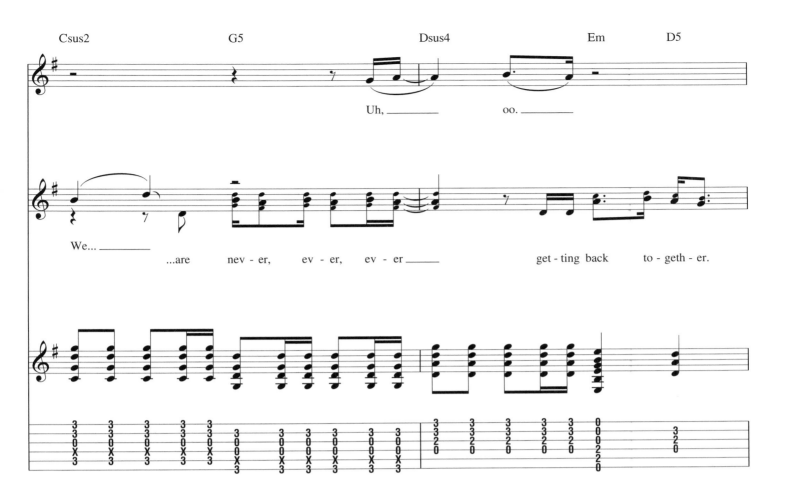

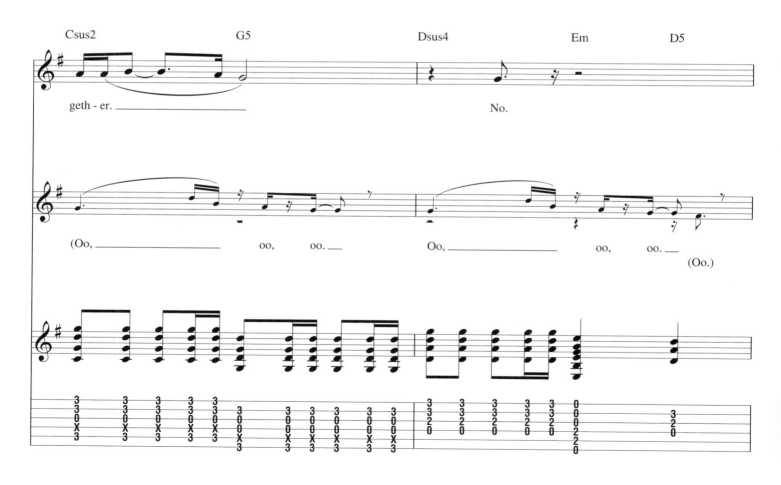

HAL•LEONARD GUITAR PLAY-ALONG

This series will help you play your favorite songs quickly and easily. Just follow the tab and listen to the CD to the hear how the guitar should sound, and then play along using the separate backing tracks. Mac or PC users can also slow down the tempo without changing pitch by using the CD in their computer. The melody and lyrics are included in the book so that you can sing or simply follow along.

Complete song lists available online.

Prices, contents, and availability subject to change without notice.

HAL•LEONARD® CORPORATION

7777 W. BLUEMOUND RD. P.O. BOX 13819 MILWAUKEE, WI 53213

www.halleonard.com